But Can't Anybody Pray?

What Makes Workplace Prayer Special?

A.J. Lykosh, Bob Perry

Makarios Press

Copyright © 2024 by A.J. Lykosh and Bob Perry

978-1-956561-59-3

All rights reserved.

No portion of this book may be reproduced in any form without written permission from the publisher or author, except as permitted by U.S. copyright law.

The most underutilized source of spiritual power in our churches today is intercession for Christian leaders. ~ C. Peter Wagner

Contents

Introduction 1

The Gift and Definition of Intercession

    1. Let's Go for a Dozen 7

    2. The Gift of Intercession 11

    3. Intercession Defined 15

    4. Stewarding the Gift 21

    5. One Specific, Unexpected Type of Intercessor 25

The Need for Intercession

    6. The Need for Prayer Coverage 31

    7. The Biblical Instruction 37

    8. Outsourcing Prayer 41

    9. Do We See Prayer Coverage in the Scriptures? 47

    10. A Historical Example 51

    11. Come Be Activated in Prayer 53

Conclusion 57

Prayer Support 61

Introduction

A month after first meeting Bob Perry, I asked him, "What makes you so special that you are a paid intercessor? Why can I not just pray on my own and avoid the whole messy payment aspect?"

Bob's answer to come in a bit, but in the meantime, to clarify: at that time, I had experienced weeks of the increased power and authority of Bob's prayers.

And yet, I still wondered: shouldn't everyone be able to pray?

The answer is: yes and no.

Or, perhaps: what do you mean by "pray"?

Some people carry greater authority in prayer.

Some people have a gift or a grace to pray. An hour in prayer is not equal for all believers. For some, that's a tremendously long time. For others, it's just getting started.

Some people choose to study prayer, to keep growing in their gift.

Then, even for those with the gift to pray, some people carry a specific grace in a particular direction. Elizabeth Alves talks about different types of intercessors, including financial intercessors.

Which is to say: I had a lot to learn.

This book satisfies my curiosity and answers my questions.

The Gift and Definition of Intercession

Chapter 1

Let's Go for a Dozen

My parents started a business in 1990. From the beginning, we had prayer time, on the clock, for the staff. Paid prayer has always been part of their company culture.

In 2020, they hired Bob Perry, a professional intercessor, someone who has spent 40 years saying, "Lord, teach me to pray."

I was curious to see if anything would change. After all, Sonlight Curriculum had a 30 year history of prayer, and truly miraculous, supernatural protection already.

Our extended family started with Bob on June 1, 2020.

On June 3, I texted him at 11pm. "Bob! We've had ten answered prayers *today!*"

I thought this was the best news ever. I was practically turning cartwheels.

He texted me back: "Let's go for a dozen."

And I remember looking at my phone, wondering, "Are you kidding me? It's 11pm! You think we're going to get two more answered prayers in the next hour?"

And then I thought, "Wow. More than anyone I've ever met, Bob *really* believes that prayer works."

We did get to a dozen that day, which was amazing.

And then, for the rest of the month, my extended family didn't see less than a dozen answered prayers any day.

We had some days where we hit two dozen, and at least one day where we hit 27 answered prayers.[1]

That experience showed me that there is a difference between prayer with sincere believers, as my parents had had for thirty years, and those who were trained in prayer, like Bob.

He has such a deep faith that what he prays will make a difference.

And because of his training and experience, he carries an uncommon authority.

Not All Prayer Is Prayer

Growing up, I would have defined prayer as talking to God.

---

1. I document this incredible outpouring in *Burning Bushes Everywhere*.

And on some level, that's correct, but I also realize now that two people can use the same word, even though it doesn't mean the same thing.

Matthew 7:28-29, at the end of the Sermon on the Mount, says: "When Jesus had finished saying these things, the crowds were amazed at his teaching, because he taught as one who had authority, and not as their teachers of the law."[2]

The teachers of the law were teaching, and Jesus was teaching.

But they weren't doing the same thing.

Jesus's teaching was *substantively* different. His words carried different authority, the Greek word *exousia*. Other translations of *exousia*: his words carried a different power, right, liberty, jurisdiction, strength; force, capacity, competency, freedom, mastery; the power of him whose will and commands must be submitted to by others and obeyed.

Jesus and the teachers of the law, on the surface, seemed to be doing the same thing, but they were not actually the same.

I was reminded of this comparison when I first heard Bob Perry pray.

I thought, "Oh! In prayer, this man is like Moses. He talks to God and expects God to answer him!"

Before I met Bob, I prayed as best I knew how. I'm sure I prayed good words, and I know God saw me as a beloved

---

2. Almost identical wording also in Mark 1:22.

daughter. I was obedient, but with no sense of force or effectiveness. I had no expectation that what I prayed would come to pass.

But I've been growing.

Now when I pray, I do so with a sense of power and authority. I *expect* a change to happen.

So when we talk about prayer, that's what we mean, but I don't know that expectant prayer is a standard perspective on prayer.

Chapter 2

The Gift of Intercession

When I first met Bob's friend Paul Van Hoesen, he kept saying, "A.J., not everyone can do what you do."

I didn't get it. My own route to prayer was so circuitous—including eight years of almost no prayer—that I figured almost anyone *could* pray.

It wasn't until some years later, when I read the late C. Peter Wagner's book *Prayer Shield*, that Wagner clarified some basic erroneous assumptions I had, which helped explained Paul's statement.

In the scriptures, three main New Testament passages talk about the gifts of the Spirit.[1]

---

1. Romas 12, I Corinthians 12, and Ephesians 4

None of the three lists is complete in itself—there is significant overlap. Some gifts are mentioned in one list only, some in two, and some in all three. A composite of the three lists gives us a 20 gifts: prophecy, service, teaching, exhortation, giving, leadership, mercy, wisdom, knowledge, faith, healings, miracles, discerning of spirits, tongues, interpretation of tongues, apostle, helps, administration, evangelist and pastor.

Five additional spiritual gifts are mentioned in the New Testament apart from the three major lists. They include: celibacy (I Cor. 7:7), voluntary poverty (I Cor. 13:3), hospitality (I Pet. 4:9-10), martyrdom (I Cor. 13:3), and missionary (Eph. 3:6-9). This gives us a total of 25 spiritual gifts listed as such in the New Testament.

... If none of the three major lists of spiritual gifts is complete in itself, and if the composite of the three is not complete either, could it be that the total of 25 gifts mentioned as such in the New Testament is also an open-ended list? If so, might there be some spiritual gifts operative in the body y of Christ that are not directly labeled as gifts in the New Testament?[2]

Wagner added three more gifts to the list.

One was deliverance, the ability to recognize evil spirits when they're at work, and bind them and cast them out. This is a part of the ministry of Jesus, healing prayer, and some traditions of healing.

The second was the ability to lead worship. This is not the same as musically gifted. Many people have beautiful voices, but not all musicians have the ability to usher others into the presence of the Lord in music.

And the third was the gift of intercession.

Before he defined intercession—coming up next—he pointed out something that, in retrospect, is obvious, but wasn't obvious to me prior: every gift is in the minority.

In the physical body, we recognize this: more parts of the body are not the eyes than are the eyes. More parts of the body are not the hands than are the hands.

Likewise with spiritual gifts: more people are not pastors than are pastors. More people are not evangelists than are evangelists.

Every one of the gifts is a minority.

---

2. *Prayer Shield*, p. 39

Of course, just because we don't have a *gift* doesn't mean we avoid the need entirely.

Even without the gift of teaching, most parents teach their children to tie their shoes.

Even without the gift of giving, most Christians give something, at least sometimes.

Even without the gift of evangelism, we are supposed to be ready to give the reason for the hope that is in us with meekness and fear.

Even without the gift of hospitality, we invite people to share our lives.

We put into practice these good behaviors, even if we don't have the gift.

Similarly with prayer: all believers should pray, but some people have a greater gift to be able to do so.

Bob's and my friend David Fitzpatrick had an extended period of several years where the Lord called him to pray eight hours a day. He said later: "I asked the Lord once why more people did not pray more. And he said, 'I don't require everyone to pastor. And I don't require everyone to see. But I do require my seers to see.'"

Use the gift that you have been given.

Chapter 3

Intercession Defined

Wagner offered a beautiful definition of intercession.

> The gift of intercession is a special ability that God gives to certain members of the Body of Christ to pray for extended periods of time on a regular basis, experience a special intimacy with God, and see frequent and specific answers to their prayers to a degree much greater than that which is expected of the average Christian.[1]

Intercessors cry out on behalf of others.

Intercessors resonate with the words of Isaiah 62:6-7: "I have posted watchmen on your walls, Jerusalem; they will nev-

---

1. *Prayer Shield*, p. 46

er be silent day or night. You who call on the Lord, give yourselves no rest, and give him no rest till he establishes Jerusalem and makes her the praise of the earth."

The intercessors keep watch. They defend against threats, and they do so day and night.

They cry out to God without rest, and give God no rest, because they yearn for God to act in accordance with his will.

Wagner goes on to give some observations from his own research:

- They pray longer. One hour per day is the minimum I've encountered; more typically, they pray two to five hours per day.
- They pray with more intensity. For many, their prayer time is often an emotional experience involving both laughter and tears.
- They achieve a sense of intimacy with God—a familiarity that allows them to hear from God and see through God's eyes for any circumstances He chooses.
- They have a greater faith to know that they are praying in God's will, and that the will of God is going to be accomplished.
- They enjoy prayer more and receive more personal satisfaction from their prayer times.

- They see more frequent and dramatic answers to their prayers. This raises their faith and provides more fuel for the fires of intercession that burn within them.
- They are acutely aware of hearing clearly and directly from God. Many have both the gift of intercession and the gift of prophecy. I have observed a significant overlap between these two gifts.[2]

As I read, I felt a shock of recognition, as, in point after point, he clearly defined my lived experience.

Wagner would estimate that, like many of the gifts, somewhere between 5% and 10% of believers carry the gift of intercession.

He emphasized that we need to not project our gifts onto others. Our gifts feel effortless to us ... because we carry these gifts!

But just because I love to pray doesn't mean that I should assume that everyone else should love it as much as I do. If I find it easy and pleasant to pray for hours a day, I shouldn't assume that everyone else ought to pray that much, too.

And while I mentally assented to this, it wasn't until I read Wagner's description of his own prayer life that this idea of projecting our gift onto others really sank in.

---

2. *Ibid.*, pp. 46-47

First Wagner said that he was inspired to set an hour a day for prayer as his (eventual) goal. "[M]any years later, I can say I have left the 22 minutes behind.[3] I pray more than 30 minutes on most days, and occasionally more than 40. But one hour? It is still a life goal, and I may make it someday. But not yet. One hour is a really long time for prayer! At least, it is in my mind."

He next described the first time he prayed for one hour. He had gone to David Yonggi Cho's church in South Korea, the largest church in the world at the time, and Cho offered to take him to Yoido Church Prayer Mountain.

I had never visited the prayer mountain, so I jumped at the chance, looking forward to a personal tour. When we arrived, I began wondering when the tour would begin. However, Cho—of all things—simply said, "Now let's pray!" Pray? I would have preferred walking around and taking pictures of others who were praying, but naturally I kept my thoughts to myself. Then he added, "We really don't have much time. Let's pray this afternoon for only one hour!"

I wanted to be a good sport. So I sat there on the floor of the huge chapel (Korean style) and started to pray. I prayed for what felt like quite a long time, and then I looked at my watch.

---

3. The average number of minutes that the average pastor prays per day.

I thought my watch had stopped! That turned out to be one of the longest hours I can remember spending. Time went faster when my wife was in labor!"[4]

I found this so helpful. I daily trek down to the lower pasture and walk for an hour, talking to the Lord. I cry and I laugh and I dance and I sit. Sometimes I pray in tongues and sometimes I sing and sometimes I'm silent. Whatever feels right.

But that time almost never feels long to me. Some days definitely seem to take longer than others, but on balance, an hour is just not that much time.

Oh! Because I'm an intercessor. I have a gift to pray.

This is what my friend Paul meant when he said, "Not everyone can do what you do."

Between all my prayer time (calls with Bob and our larger team, as well as in the lower pasture), I walk, in the course of the year, an average of about 19,000 steps per day. Minimum 10,000, but averaging almost twice that. At my rate of walking, that's about three hours a day, day in and day out.

---

4. *Ibid.*, pp. 94-95

Bob's average is about 40,000 steps per day. He walks and prays, then, six or seven hours a day. A five hour prayer hike for him is like a shower: a regular refreshment.[5]

But my point is: I hadn't considered that even my quantity of prayer time was anything special. (Bob's, though? Clearly unusual!)

So Wagner's story was such a helpful reminder that most people find even an hour to pray to be a long time.

The Lord gives some a gift to pray longer than others, and that longer prayer time is not a burden, but an eager volunteer thing. Sign me up!

I know Bob and I experimented with taking Sundays off instead of praying together. After a few weeks, we stopped, because we missed that time too much.

Which is to say: the gift, the practice, of intercession takes time.

If your lane is to own a business, then own a business.

If your lane is to work, then work.

We celebrate all the gifts that the Holy Spirit gives to the body.

To partner with intercessors simply acknowledges that we have different gifts.

---

5. Walking, of course, isn't required of an intercessor. Most intercessors we know stay inside during their prayer times.

Chapter 4

Stewarding the Gift

Before I met Bob, I had never really thought that we can practice prayer and seek to improve.

I hadn't realized that we could actually study prayer, and that, as we dedicate ourselves to our craft, we can become more effective.

And yet, in the natural realm, we know that what we practice well, we improve.

Think of a young beginning peewee football player. That child is not going to be as talented or skilled as Tom Brady, with his seven Super Bowl wins.

Ideally, both the peewee football player and Tom Brady bask in their fathers' love, and their value with their fathers does not depend on their talent on the ball field.

But in terms of their efficacy in getting the job done, Tom Brady was more effective because he has honed his abilities. He spent the time. He worked the hours. He figured out the plays. He endured the practices. He refined his ability to mentally shut off whatever disappointment may have happened in the last play and look ahead to the next. He had the capacity to come through in the clutch moments.

Presumably he also had great natural ability, and the stature and the brain power and the drive to nurture and steward his abilities to a high level.

A few other examples: we recognize that musicians who practice perform better, that post-graduate mathematicians know more than kindergarteners first starting addition, that Michelin-star chefs have greater facility than young people boiling noodles for the first time.

None of this is offensive. It's simply common sense.

Moving from the natural to the spiritual, we also recognize that teachers and evangelists can become better at what they do, and that prophets can learn to listen more clearly to what the Lord is saying.[1]

For many years, I missed that this was also true in prayer.

But then I met Bob who, for 40 years, has had the single-minded cry of his heart: "Lord, teach me to pray."

---

1. In one conference around the prophetic, I loved how several speakers spoke on what the Lord was teaching them *now*. What new things was he asking them to try?

Since prayer is effective, of course he would actually have more ability to be able to pray effectively.

As he has spent decades of focused intention reading and practicing, experimenting and learning, attending conferences and trying new ideas, seeking the presence of God and effective partnership with other believers, he is actually more effective in prayer than those who haven't invested in prayer in the same way.

Bob said, early on, "I have 500 books on prayer in my library, all about how to change the world. My wife Sharon has 500 books on prayer in her library, all about *Lectio Divina* and contemplation. We both love prayer, but we pray in different ways."

In his Strength Finder survey, he was high in competition, so he studied how to pray for results.

As such, he has more tools in his tool belt to be able to pull out at any given time. He has prayed the scriptures for decades, and he hears from God in many different ways.

He has honed his capacity.

Two people with a similar gifting don't exercise that gifting in the same way. Some people take their time and their resources and seek out training and impartation. They practice and grow in expertise. They steward the gift.

Not all do.

But when someone has taken their time and effort and resources to gain expertise and hone their craft in prayer, their prayers have a different intensity and power.

Chapter 5

One Specific, Unexpected Type of Intercessor

Elizabeth Alves, in her book *Intercessors*, wrote about 14 different types of prayers that different people feel called to pray.

Prayers for their nation. Disaster relief. Worship. Salvation for those not yet in the fold.

These all made sense. I had seen them in practice.

But one type caught my attention: the financial intercessor.

I had never heard of this. And yet, according to Alvez, some people receive from the Lord the gift that, when they pray for increase, it happens.[1]

When I read this description, I had a shock of recognition. *This is Bob Perry!*

I called him and said, "Bob! This is you! When you pray for businesses, the businesses see tremendous increase!"

He had read *Intercessors* about 20 years before, perhaps 15 years before he started to pray for businesses. He had forgotten this type of intercessor even existed.

Yet he sees such dramatic results.

A few examples from when we were starting Workplace Prayer, in the nine month period from mid-2020 to early 2021.

- The 51-year-old company that suddenly had record-breaking sales, week after week, despite the chaotic challenges of that time of global disruption.

- The business with stagnant sales for a decade or so, that suddenly doubled in the months after he started praying.

- The family that was already earning a comfortable income, when the dad suddenly got a 25% raise.

---

1. She notes that this doesn't usually work for the person praying for themselves. You can't identify financial intercessors as the billionaires in the room. But they can pray for *others* and see increase.

- The business with an ongoing legal battle for three years, that, a month or two after partnering with Workplace Prayer, suddenly resolved completely in favor of the client, who took home $35,000.

When Bob prays for businesses, things actually shift. That's not something that he put in himself. That's a gift that the Lord gives him.

And Bob carries his gift to the wider world.

Two basic points.

1) If you haven't ever prayed for increase for your business ... start! You might be a financial intercessor and not know it!

The book of James says, "You have not because you ask not."

My mom realized that, for 30 years, she had requests for her customers, she had been asking for her vendors, she had been asking for the children, she had been asking for the staff. But she said, "I never once asked for increase. We are actually doing good in the world! We're seeking to bring God's kingdom! Why would I not want my brand and my products to spread to the places where they're needed? But I didn't even think about it."

But once she realized she could ask, she started to ask.

And 2) if you have a business, or work in a business that you would like to see prosper, we are happy to pray for you.

It is our joy to pray into the bigger and better things that the business owners themselves might be afraid to ask for.

The Need for Intercession

Chapter 6

The Need for Prayer Coverage

In C. Peter Wagner's first edition of *Prayer Shield*, he focused on how pastors need prayer coverage.

His research showed that pastors prayed an average of 22 minutes a day. Some, obviously, prayed longer, and some prayed shorter.

These are pastors, people who have been trained in the ways of the Lord, shepherding their flocks ... praying 22 minutes out of the 1,440 minutes every day.

In the end: he recommended that pastors intentionally try to get to 22 minutes, because things actually do go better with prayer.

But his main point was that pastors need to do the work of pastoring ... but they can still be covered in prayer, when they partner with an intercessor, or an intercessory team.

In his revised edition, he no longer focused exclusively on pastors, but had come a more expansive view of the church: as he described it, the nuclear church (Sunday morning service), and the extended church (the saints in the workplace).

He wrote:

> [W]e are now recognizing that what God assigns his people to do in the workplace is just as valid a form of Christian ministry. This change in thinking, as you can imagine, involves a major paradigm shift....
>
> Our new paradigm suggests, however, that the leaders God has given to the Church will be found in all seven mountains,[1] not just the Religion Mountain.[2]

He basically said: most of what I write will apply to any leader. Please extrapolate for yourself.

And while I agree with what he says about leaders, I also recognize that the reasons below can apply to a wide range of people.

---

1. Also called "spheres of influence": family, religion, education, media, entertainment, business, and government.

2. *Prayer Shield*, p. 58

Some want prayer coverage because they are caretakers for parents and dealing with troubled children. Some work in difficult environments, and aren't sure of the way forward from within the organization. (At the top, you can set the trajectory more easily than from the middle.)

So while these reasons use the language of "leaders," please extrapolate to your own field. A leader might be the visionary who is starting a business, or a sister who wants to see change in the family business, or a stay-at-home mom who wants her husband to flourish.

For any and all leaders, then, here is my paraphrase of Wagner's reasons why a leader might want a prayer shield.

1) Being a leader is costly.

2) Leaders are "more beat up than you think." Outside expectations can wear us down.

3) Leaders need help. Yes. Wagner originally pointed out: where would a pastor go for help?

But as my friend Emma expanded the need: "If you're an executive, where are you going to go for help and support? You are supposed to have it all together."

4) An epidemic of failing leaders.

Wagner emphasizes the difficulties for pastors, such as burnout and sexual immorality.

Though these might be issues for anyone, the main marketplace challenges look a bit different: lack of capital, poor management, poor planning, and ineffective marketing.[3]

Perhaps we could adjust this fourth idea to simply: the constant risk of failure.

While I don't disagree with Wagner on any of these points—costliness, wear and tear, lack of support, and the constant threat of failure—aren't these issues for most people?

Why might leaders, specifically, want a prayer shield?

1) Leaders have more responsibility and accountability.

2) Leaders are more subject to temptation. In the business world, we understand the challenges: travel away from home. Seductive intentions from people who want to be close to power. The need to blow off the stress of carrying the weight of responsibility.

3) Leaders are more often targets of warfare.

Dr. Francis MacNutt first brought this to my attention, when, in a training on healing prayer, he said this: So I listened with fascination and horror to Francis MacNutt teach on deliverance. He said, "We have 63 active covens in Jacksonville. We know that they target us and our ministry by name. They

---

3. https://www.investopedia.com/articles/personal-finance/120815/4-most-common-reasons-small-business-fails.asp

have their feasts, and they get together to do mischief during the full moon. Ever notice the oddities that happen at the full moon? It's not the moon that affects people, but the witches."

Wagner shared his own story, of his friend, John Vaughn of the International Church Research Center. John was flying to Boston, and the man next to him appeared to pray.

When he finished, John casually asked, "Are you a Christian?" The man had no way of knowing that Vaughn himself was a Christian, a Baptist pastor and a university professor.

He seemed shocked by the question and replied, "Oh, no. You have me all wrong. I'm not a Christian; I'm actually a satanist!"

John then asked him what he was praying for as a satanist.

The man said, "Do you really want to know?"

When John affirmed that he did, the satanist replied, "My primary attention is directed toward the fall of Christian pastors and their families living in New England."...

This encounter made John realize just how essential intercession for pastors really is. Did Christians take time to pray for their pastors in New England that day? Whose prayer was answered—the Christians' or the satanists's?

As humans, we deal with passive resistance ... and surely there's plenty of that. Interrupted sleep, a grumpy clerk, lack of attention to detail, and a hundred other petty problems.

But anyone in a position to seek to do good can meet active resistance as well: the specific, intentional, literal cursing of the work of God.

4) Leaders have influence over a larger number of people. As such, more people are affected by what the leader does.

5) Leaders have more visibility. People notice what the leader is doing and talk about it.

Which is all to say: Wagner's book basically says: if you're a leader, yes, you should pray. At least a few minutes a day. (If you're not, then start.)

But the reality is: unless you're also called to be an intercessor, most leaders and business owners are so busy running their business, they don't have the time or the energy to also dive deep into how to pray effectively.

We all need prayer, though.

So get prayer coverage.

Chapter 7

The Biblical Instruction

In Ephesians 6, Paul describes the Armor of God. Eugene Peterson's *The Message* gives a fresh look at these familiar verses.

And that about wraps it up. God is strong, and he wants you strong. So take everything the Master has set out for you, well-made weapons of the best materials. And put them to use so you will be able to stand up to everything the Devil throws your way. This is no weekend war that we'll walk away from and forget about in a couple of hours. This is for keeps, a life-or-death fight to the finish against the Devil and all his angels.

Be prepared. You're up against far more than you can handle on your own. Take all the help you can get, every weapon God has issued, so that when it's all over but the shouting you'll still be on your feet. Truth, righteousness, peace, faith, and salvation are more than words. Learn how to apply them. You'll need them throughout your life. God's Word is an indispensable weapon. In the same way, prayer is essential in this ongoing warfare. Pray hard and long. Pray for your brothers and sisters. Keep your eyes open. Keep each other's spirits up so that no one falls behind or drops out.

In any given week, as we talk to different friends and clients, we're reminded again and again how much sadness and pain we all carry. Broken marriages, broken work environments, broken relationships, broken health, broken systems, broken lives, broken dreams.

You're up against far more than you can handle on your own.

If we sometimes find it hard to keep your head above water, no shame there.

This is for keeps, a life-or-death fight to the finish against the Devil and all his angels.

And yet, despite the direness of Paul's statement ... God gives us help. We have a chance to stand on our feet.

Pray hard and long. Pray for your brothers and sisters. Keep your eyes open. Keep each other's spirits up so that no one falls behind or drops out.

At Workplace Prayer, we pray hard and long, because we know that we're all up against far more than we can handle on our own.

Chapter 8

Outsourcing Prayer

My friend (and now Workplace Prayer client) Kristin, an executive for a food service company, explained outsourcing to me.

You outsource things for two reasons.

The first is for things that are so unique, and so specialized, that it's easier to have someone else do it because it's not the core of your business.

Think of corporate dining, companies that offer lunch and catering.

In 2008, during the peak of the recession, this large defense company still did their food service in-house. The lunch ladies were getting the same benefits as the people who were making the stealth planes.

The defense company came under such business pressure, that the question was literally, "Would you rather keep your rocket scientists or your lunch ladies?"

They decided to give their lunch ladies to someone who would care for them. In a time of ridiculous business pressure, it made their decision clear, while previously it had not been clear.

One reason people outsource is to allow a business to focus on their core competency, which also usually results in cost savings.

The second reason to outsource is for the specialization.

I wake up and think about how to serve you lunch. All day long, that's the only thing I think about. This is my passion and my love.

I've seen it done in hundreds of different way. So when you have a problem, I've probably seen it already.

Outsource things that aren't your core competency? And that involve specialized knowledge?

Prayer fits this description.

But what does it mean to outsource prayer?

In Wagner's life, he prayed as he felt led. He pushed himself to pray 22 minutes a day, and then went up from there.

But he had a team of intercessors behind him to pray longer and more intensively.

In the natural realm, we recognize the idea of shared responsibility.

Most businesses outsource their tax preparation, for example. The business owner still holds the responsibility for the numbers submitted to the tax preparer, and the responsibility for the overall filing, but the accountant does the majority of the work.

In the case of Kristin's food service, the assisted living director dictates the menu direction the residents require (Kosher, for example). The director holds the responsibility, even while turning the details over to someone else.

In the case of prayer, the Workplace Prayer team has spent years learning and training and growing in prayer. Conferences and workshops, trainings and impartations. So those who partner with us pray, and we pray, too.

With any outsourcing, the critical issue seems to be *responsibility*.

When we hire others to pray, we are still responsible for our own walk with God.

But, like a tax preparer, at Workplace Prayer, trained prayer people come alongside, in their area of expertise, to offer support.

As Kristin said in that first meeting: "The business climate is not getting better. We need someone like you serving alongside us."

We All Outsource ... But We Don't Outsource Everything

As we walk with God, we each have direct access to him, and we have support people.

Some things I have to do for myself: no one else can worship God on my behalf. No one else can thank him for what he's done for me. No one else can hear his instructions to me, nor obey them.

I need to spend time with God on my own, cultivating my own ability to hear his voice. I need to ask him questions and listen for his answers.

But that's not the sum total of my walk of faith.

I know that I hear God's voice, but I still appreciate prophetic declarations over my life, reminding me of my identity, calling me to bigger picture thinking, offering unexpected suggestions.

I am grateful for my own experience, but I like teachers to help put words to what I'm noticing.[1]

I know that I'm reasonably good at prayer, but I still appreciate Bob's powerful prayer, especially on the days when I am struggling.

I remind God of my needs, but I treasure the prayer team that stands with me.

---

1. As with Wagner's description of an intercessor in Chapter 3.

While I have been trained in healing prayer, I appreciate the healing prayer minister who helps me make sense of my life.

I appreciate all who have taught and mentored me, and continue to do so.

I have my part in the journey, and I have others come alongside to help support and buoy my walk of faith.

I am grateful for every part that contributes to the fullness of life, the *shalom* of God.

Chapter 9

Do We See Prayer Coverage in the Scriptures?

Although I had noticed plenty of examples of prayer in the scripture—Esther, Nehemiah, Daniel—Wagner pointed out two more that I hadn't noticed.

Early in the book of Acts, James was put to death and Peter was arrested, about to be killed. But "constant prayer was offered for him by the church."[1]

Peter experienced a miraculous escape from the high security Antonia Prison, and went to the prayer meeting: "the house belonging to Mary, the mother of John Mark.... She had done what any responsible personal intercessor would have done in the midst of such happenings. She immediately got in touch

---

1. Acts 12:5

with as many other intercessors as she could, and invited them to her home for a lengthy prayer vigil. How powerful was their prayer? Peter's life was spared, and Herod ended up being eaten by worms (see Acts 12:23)![2]

And then the apostle Paul. He not only requested prayer generally ("pray for us"),[3] but also requested prayer for specific needs (like getting out of jail: "I trust that through your prayers I shall be granted to you").[4]

Paul also talked about two women who, Paul says "labored with me in the gospel," Euodia and Syntyche.[5]

Commentator F. F. Bruce notes that the Greek word verb translated "labored with me in the gospel" is a very strong verb, *synathleo*.

> [This word means] they "contended" or "strived" or "fought at my side." Edmond Hiebert says the term "implies united action in the face of opposition and strife," so Paul's metaphor "pic-

---

2. *Prayer Shield*, p. 30

3. I Thessalonians 5:25

4. Philemon 1:22

5. Philippians 4:3 (NKJV), prononounced something like: *you OH dee uh* and *sin TICK ee*.

tures these women as having served Paul's fellow soldiers in the battle to establish the gospel in Philippi." This is the language of intercession of spiritual warfare, which is exactly the way that F.W. Beare sees it. He argues that these two courageous women were "pitted along with Paul 'against principalities and powers ... against the spiritual hosts of wickedness in the heavenly places' of Ephesians 6:12."[6]

Wagner believes that a more explicit translation would be, "*They did* spiritual warfare *on my behalf.*"[7]

So, yes, we do see prayer coverage exercising earnest prayer on behalf of leaders.[8]

---

6. *Prayer Shield*, p. 31

7. *Ibid.*, emphasis in the original

8. So far as we can tell ... none of these prayer people were compensated. So where does payment fit in? We deal with that question in our book *The Ethics of Paying for Prayer*.

Chapter 10

A Historical Example

As part of my boys' homeschooling, every few years I read Janet and Geoff Benge's biography, *George Muller: The Guardian of Bristol's Orphans*.

Muller founded orphanages in Bristol, England, and funded them through prayer.

In one memorable scene, the children thanked God for their breakfast, though the orphanage had no food at all. When the prayer ended, a knock came at the door. A baker had started baking at 2am, compelled to make sure the orphans had food.

As he carried in his loaves, another knock came. The milk cart had broken down right in front of the orphanage. In order to fix the cart, the milkman needed to lighten the load, and asked if the orphans could please drink the milk, instead of him simply dumping it out.

Decades of stories of provision like these.

But after starting Workplace Prayer, one quote leaped out afresh for me.

"Before [Muller] would feel comfortable leaving Bristol, there needed to be at least 200 pounds in the bank so the staff would not have to take on the responsibility of praying for the day-to-day operating expenses."[1]

Muller knew that he needed to pray so his staff could do their work.

The staff were, presumably, godly people, working well.

But they didn't *all* pray constantly for God's provision.

That was George Muller's responsibility, so that the work could go on.

This is not an exact corollary of paying for prayer for business, but I appreciate the practical differentiation: some do the work, and some provide prayer coverage.

---

1. p. 138

Chapter 11

Come Be Activated in Prayer

A ndy Mason, founder of Heaven in Business and Workplace Prayer client, once offered an insightful comment.

So many business owners outsource their authority to somebody else: their pastor, their wife, their husband, whoever is the spiritual one.

It is not acceptable. Like zero.

So I've been super resistant about any organization that says, "I do the prophetic for you. I do this for you. I do that for you" ... *unless* they actually equip and train and activate their people in the process.

That's their job.

That's why I love Bob and A.J., because they won't just pray *for* you, they pray *with* you.

And you will learn to pray and be sucked into their vortex. They'll actually train you.

That's their job!

Any organization that does not do that? Don't engage with it. It's not worth your money.

We do take the training and equipping seriously.

Bob had been sending weekly prayers for years before I met him.

When we met, I had been emailing daily for months already, and within a year, started podcasting.

Even if you only spend five minutes a day in prayer ... we want those five minutes to be effective and powerful.

Here's where you can find some of our free equipping and training.

Bob's weekly email: praybig.me/prayer

My daily email: praybig.me/email

The Make Prayer Beautiful Podcast: amyjoy.me/podcast

Come be activated in prayer.

Conclusion

A month after first meeting Bob, I asked him, "What makes you so special that you are a paid intercessor? Why can I not just pray on my own and avoid the whole messy payment aspect?"

This was Bob's answer.

Jesus and Paul talked about how the walk of faith isn't something we do alone. It's something we do in community, that we do in partnership.

This partnership perspective messes up the Western mindset of, "I'm going to do it my way, and I'm going to be independent, and I don't need anyone else."

Our culture has gone through a real shift in our thinking about independence.

You can see this in many different ways.

It used to be if you owned a car, you changed your own oil.

Today, I don't know anybody who changes their own oil. It's too difficult. It's actually cheaper to go into a shop. You have a professional who helps you, someone who is highly skilled and trained.

I think it's the same thing with prayer.

You might have a gift to lead your company or manage your sales force.

But you need a brother or sister who has been set apart by God, one who is highly skilled and trained, so they can partner with you, be that friend with you.

They can strengthen you when you are weak.

In Numbers 17, the Israelites were battling their enemies.

Young warrior Joshua went out to win the battle against the enemy, and Aaron the priest, the prayer leader, led the prayer warriors, the intercessors, along with Hur, both serving the government leader, Moses.

Aaron and Hur held up Moses' arms, and when they kept Moses' arms up in prayer, Joshua was winning the battle.

When the prayer warriors' arms got tired, or when they had to go elsewhere, or grew weary, they dropped their arms, and they dropped Moses' arms, and Joshua would begin to lose the battle.

We need prayer partnership to win. We have battles, we have obstacles, we have problems, we have crises.

We want to reach our goals. We want to reach our objectives.

The Old Testament shows that partnership between the prayer leaders and those on the front lines brought measurable victories in battle.

Joshua needed prayer support to triumph.

With prayer support, Joshua did triumph.

We want all God's children to triumph.

May the favor of the Lord our God rest on us;establish the work of our hands for us—yes, establish the work of our hands.[1]

---

1. Psalm 90:17

Prayer Support

Some years ago I asked a friend of mine about his prayer support. "I have people who pray for me."

"But do they pray more than about one sentence a week?"

"Uhhh ... I'm not sure. Tell me how I can become a client."

At Workplace Prayer, we offer prayer coverage for our clients.

We pray for our clients every day, seven days a week.

Sometimes we pray with them.

We are open to teach them how to pray more effectively.

But mostly we simply pray.

And while we welcome updates from our clients, we also know that people are busy, so whether we get updates or not, we pray.

As professional intercessors, this is what we do.

It's what we think about all day, every day.

Prayer is our joy and our privilege, and we encourage anyone in leadership, anyone in ministry, anyone in business—anyone who diligently seeks to push back the darkness—to get prayer coverage.

About the Authors

A.J. Lykosh is an author, mentor, and entrepreneur. Through Workplace Prayer, Makarios Press, the Make Prayer Beautiful podcast, and more, she covers businesses in prayer and raises up intercessors to do the same. She lives outside Charlottesville, Virginia with her husband and five sons.

Enjoy the Prayer Refresh: 21 short prayers to pray as you go about your day. praybig.me/refresh

For more than forty years, **Bob Perry**'s single request has been, "Lord, teach me to pray." After decades as an intercessor for the spheres of church and missions, he has now turned his prayer focus to the workplace community. He lives in East Nashville, Tennessee with his wife, and enjoys spending time with his four adult children.

Get his weekly prayers at praybig.biz/encouragement

Made in the USA
Middletown, DE
24 February 2024